Clown Mania

By Ed and Ruth Radlauer

AN ELK GROVE BOOK

CHILDRENS PRESS, CHICAGO

STRATEGIES, a teaching guide for using **MANIA BOOKS** for reading instruction, is available along with a cassette recording and **MANIA CARDS** (skill-builders) to accompany this book.

Photo credits:
   Robin Radlauer, pages 6, 7, 8, 29
Special thanks to these clowns:
   Betsy Boo (Betsy Brown George) p. 16
   Flash, the Sunshine Clown (Flash Messiter)
      cover, pp. 4, 15, 17, 27, 28
   Mindy (Shirley Raymond) pp. 4, 9, 26, 27, 30
   Poppins (Diane Leydecker) pp. 5, 24, 25, 31
   Graduating Clown Class, CSUSD, 1976, pp. 6, 7, 8, 29
   Rodeo Clowns:
      Walter Davis, pp. 18, 19, 22
      Duane Hargo, pp. 20, 21, 23
   Birthday Party Clowns Company
   3392 Yellowtail Drive
   Los Alamitos, CA 90720
      Bingo the Clown (Mike Lynsky) pp. 12, 13, 15, 17
      Corky the Magic Clown (Curt Wolff) pp. 10, 11, 14

Library of Congress Cataloging in Publication Data

Radlauer, Edward.
   Clown mania.

   (Mania books)
   ''An Elk Grove book.''
   SUMMARY: Uses simple vocabulary to introduce clowns.
   1. Clowns—Juvenile literature. [1. Clowns]
I. Radlauer, Ruth Shaw, joint author. II. Title.
GV1817.R32   791.3'3   80-21826
ISBN 0-516-07783-X

   2 3 4 5 6 7 8 9 10 11 12 13 14 15 R 87 86 85 84 83 82

A RADLAUER
Mania
Book

CREATED FOR CHILDRENS PRESS BY
*RADLAUER PRODUCTIONS INCORPORATED

Clown mania?
Yes, it's clown mania.

Say hello to Poppins
and Jelly Bean.

Some clowns dance.

And some clowns sing.

Do you like
white-face clowns?

To be a white-face clown,
use white-face makeup.

Use white-face makeup—

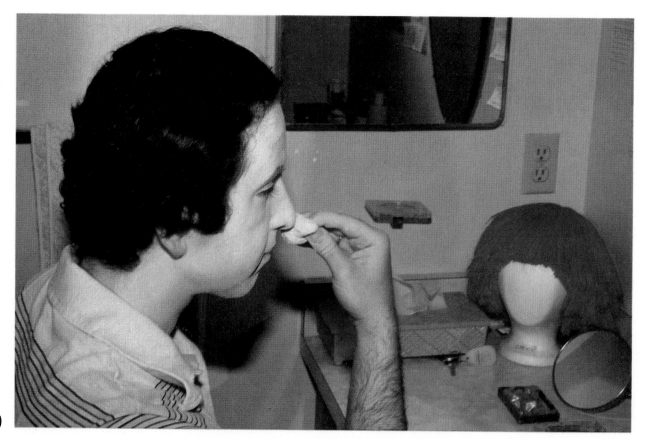

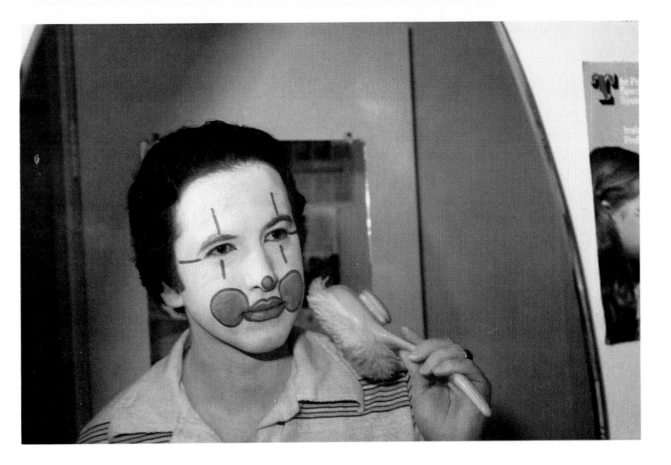

—and red makeup.

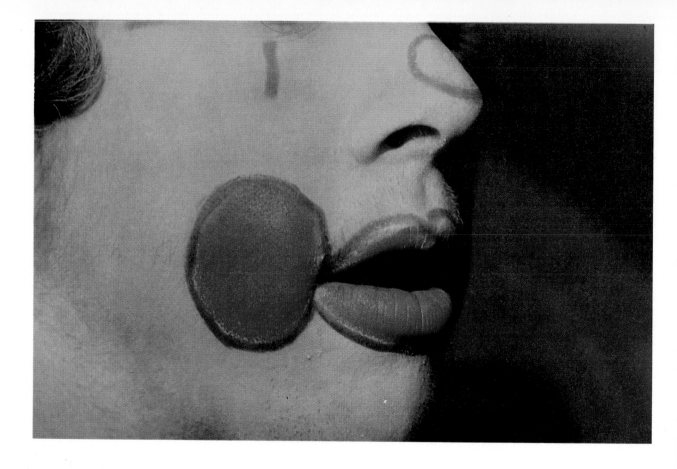

Use white-face makeup,
red makeup—

—and blue makeup.

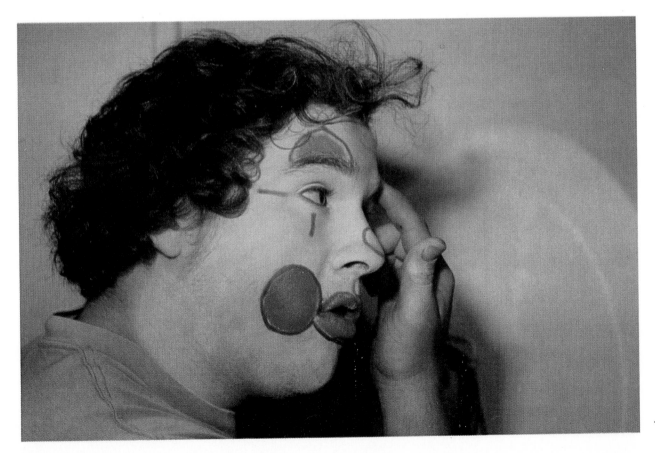

To be a clown—

—you need a wig.

You need a wig—

—and a clown suit.

A rodeo clown—

—needs a rodeo clown suit.

Rodeo clowns—

—run after the bull.

The bull—

—may run after
the rodeo clown.

Some clowns may
like red hearts—

—and white shoes
with red pompons.

Some clowns have friends—

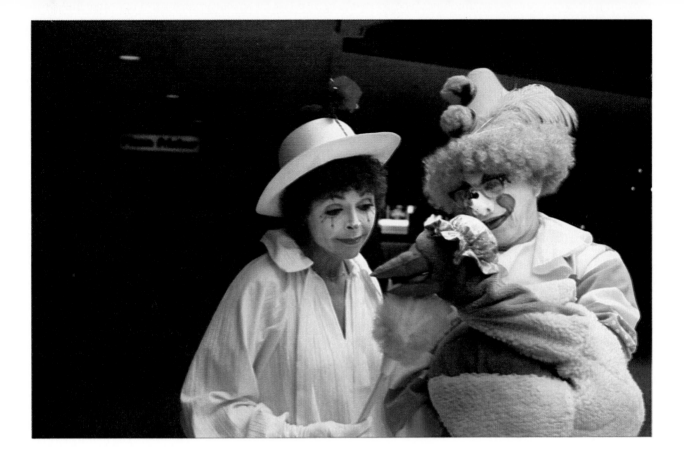

—and some friends
have clowns.

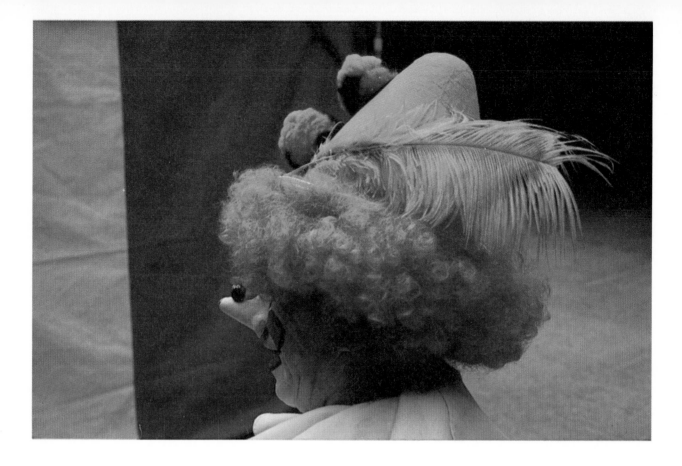

Clowns may have big hats.

Clowns may have big hats
and big shoes.

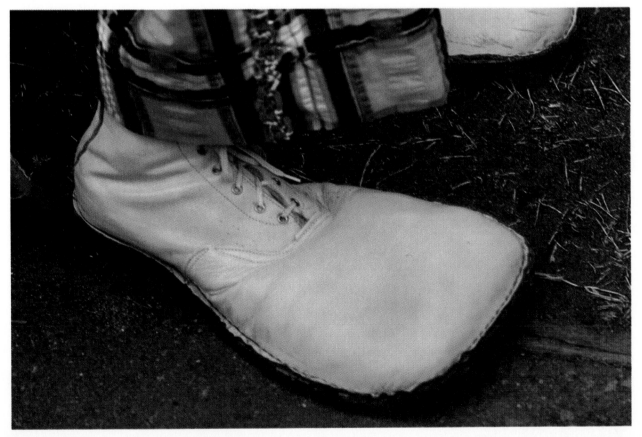

Clown mania?

Yes, it's clown mania.
Say goodbye to Poppins
and Jelly Bean.

Clown Words